CARMEL

A Timeless Place

Steve Shapiro

Publisher:

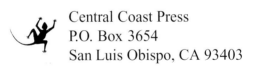

Central Coast Press
P.O. Box 3654
San Luis Obispo, CA 93403

ISBN: 0-9658776-5-5

Printed in Hong Kong

Second Printing - January 2000

All text and photographs are by Steve Shapiro

DEDICATION

This book is lovingly dedicated to my own cottage mate Patricia Tiernan Cox.

-SGS-

PREFACE

Photographing the village under the immense shadow of Edward Weston, Cole Weston, Brett Weston, Ansel Adams, Morely Bear and the great artist photographers of Group f-64 and founders of the Friends of Photography, presented an inhibiting as well as challenging task.

As a photographer who learned at the knee of those master photographers, it seems appropriate to follow through with this assignment of the heart—as an inheritor of the local legacy.

This body of photographs became a compilation of pictures of moments when light offered the Carmel village at its best. Camera angles and choices in positions were made to especially ensure the privacy of residents and keep secret the whereabouts of these intimate dwellings of both small and grand cottages. All pictures in this book were intentionally taken only from public access. These photos are meant to capture the essence of a private place.

Photographs were made with every additional effort taken to exclude specific identification of businesses except in context with Carmel's doll house architecture and gourmand taste.

* * *

While we refer to Carmel and Carmel-by-the-Sea interchangeably, some of the areas shown are actually outside of Carmel proper, which is only one square mile. Additionally, a small section south of the original city limit has been incorporated where homes have mail boxes and mail delivery.

For the purposes of this book, we have included all of these outlying areas as a part of Carmel even though they are actually under the governmental jurisdiction of Monterey County.

By the same token, we pay homage to the expansion in Carmel Woods and hope to show ideas that remain consistent with the vision of the two Franks—Devendorf and Powers.

* * *

Carmel has been blessed with such a rich history filled with notable personalities. Every building has a story to tell. Within the pages of this book, we have not attempted to include everything, but rather give the reader a basic idea of the spirit and vision which has resided in Carmel through the years. These photographs hopefully paint a picture of modern-day Carmel built upon the ideas of those who have come before.

INTRODUCTION

Gustav Stickly, an outspoken editor and critic around the turn of the century, developed an axiom for the Arts and Crafts architectural movement. He wrote about living in a highly crafted house: *"...a family that makes this their home will certainly develop traditional values of an appreciation for the long lasting, enduring emotional attachments."* Stickly inadvertently describes the town of Carmel, a timeless place.

The idea of mankind living in harmony with nature, using natural materials and conforming with the natural landscape was controversial during the early part of the 20th century. Through *The Craftsman*, an anti-industrialization magazine, Gustav Stickly became known as father of the Arts and Crafts movement.

Carmel was born and developed out of the Arts and Crafts movement. Because of this foundation upon which the town was built, one now finds a most unique place—which attracts visitors and residents from all over the world. Walking through Carmel, the visitor may notice the attention given to detail and the marriage of natural materials in both residential and commercial construction. Meandering paths and private parks as additions to the public streets invite the visitor to explore—to discover what lays around the next corner. These features invoke a sense of permanence and timelessness.

* * *

Over the years, many well known artists of every discipline have resided in Carmel. Individuals such as Mary Austin, George Sterling and Robinson Jeffers lived and thrived in this memorable coastal village among other great artists, writers, poets, critics and movie stars. A common appreciation for privacy kept them in Carmel and impelled them to protect it.

Laws aimed at protecting the residential and the private nature of the town have encouraged growth in a slow timeless manner—more in keeping with a European village.

Strict permit regulations from Carmel's earliest days have allowed secret gardens to propagate in the middle of streets. Trees boldly dominate right-of-ways; streets are divided for cars but allow trees first priority. Regulations were put in place as a purposeful effort to save the unusual coastal flora that comes from as far away as China as well as rare indigenous species.

Because of the garden-like nature of Carmel streets, visitors sometimes become disoriented while driving and parking in town. Even longtime residents have been known to forget the whereabouts of their cars while parked in town.

Modern concepts of commerce have sometimes been in conflict with the ethics of the village residential community in Carmel-by-the-Sea. Disputes involving businesses have consistently erupted through the years as Carmel residents have fought to find the best way to maintain their long term ideals. With artists as politicians, ingenious local laws bent and sometimes broke after each election...but the changes almost always supported the natural surroundings and boosted ecological preservation.

The resulting town consists of quaint houses of strong character. The success of creative people attracted others who brought their families. Bungalows as playhouses became weekend cottages and then early retirement getaways. Creative minds brought creative construction and ingenious remodeling. Community interest and support for the arts is as strong as it is deeply rooted in Carmel's past. The area has been blessed with a rich architectural and historical heritage that can be traced back to its very earliest days.

EARLY HISTORY

The first inhabitants of the Monterey Peninsula were believed to be the Ohlone Indians whose villages dotted the shores of Monterey Bay. The region was rich in natural resources and food. Ohlone religion treated the natural environment as sacred. Prayers and rituals developed to encourage balance and peace between people and the elements.

One of the first European explorers of the California central coast was Juan Rodríguez Cabrillo, who in 1542 anchored near Monterey Bay (historians disagree whether Cabrillo actually anchored in Monterey Bay) and claimed the area for Spain.

In 1602, the ambitious and adventurous explorer Sebastián Vizcaíno arrived. The captain of a Spanish exploratory galleon set anchor in a small, calm bay off the coast of California. Vizcaíno noticed the Carmel River and wetlands as they embraced the sea. Because Vizcaíno was accompanied by three friars of the Carmelite order, (a monastic order originating from Mount Carmel in the Holy Lands) he consequently named the river *El Rio del Carmelo*. Vizcaíno was so pleased with the potential of the bay as a future harbor that he named the area after the Viceroy of New Spain, Count de Monte Rey. Vizcaíno's discoveries remained long ignored. No further explorations occurred for the next 160 years.

Seeking to establish a chain of missions along the California coast, Spain sent a land expedition led by Captain Gaspar de Portolá in 1769. The group sought to find the wonderful harbor described by Vizcaíno years earlier. The explorers did not recognize the harbor and continued northwards to San Francisco Bay. On their return trip, the party set camp near present-day Carmel Bay for more than a week before resuming their journey to San Diego.

The following year, Portolá led another expedition back to Monterey Bay where he was joined by Fray Junípero Serra, president of the Franciscan missions. On June 3, 1770, Serra officially founded California's second mission...in Monterey. The mission was moved in 1771 to its present site near the mouth of the Carmel River. Father Serra's Mission San Carlos Borromeo del Rio Carmelo, built in 1772, became Carmel's first permanent building. The basilica became the area's first landmark. It was the basilica's distinctive architecture that was put on the earliest maps of Carmel.

Building in Carmel started and continued with pure belief and bold architecture. Since the construction of the basilica, unique architecture and carefully controlled land development have resulted in the memorable community that exists today.

A path to the beach passes through dense stretches of greenery and vegetation (right).

Mission San Carlos Borromeo founded in 1770.

The basilica entrance (above).

The distinctive basilica of Mission San Carlos Borromeo can be viewed from nearby residential areas.

Carmel Beach - on the western edge of Carmel

15

Development in Carmel has brought visitors from around the world. The balance between commercial and residential interests has been a contentious issue throughout Carmel's history.

CARMEL — EARLY TOWN DEVELOPMENT

Through the close of the 19th century, many cattle ranches on California's coast were developed as church communities. These properties were often considered rustic and undesirable. Many people were fearful of the coast and oceanfront property was considered a dirty place to live. The San Francisco earthquake fueled the fear about the power of nature.

As Spanish and Mexican land grants were relinquished, development rights contracts changed hands and brought about housing development. Tracts of land were commonly offered by speculators and futurists. Some were successful and some were not.

Carmel was born out of a vision by real estate agent turned developer, Frank Devendorf. During one summer (between 1888-1892), while on vacation with his wife and two daughters, the Devendorfs held a picnic on Pescadero Point, off of today's Seventeen Mile Drive. When Frank looked across Carmel Beach, he was to see the possibility for a nonsectarian, reasonably priced traditional family community. While the seeds of a vision were planted, Devendorf would wait many years before opportunity presented itself.

One of Monterey's more speculative real estate agents was Santiago Duckworth. Upon hearing of proposals by Southern Pacific Railroad to construct a railroad line to the mouth of the Carmel River, Duckworth secured an agreement from Honore Escolle (the owner) for the development of 325 acres in present-day Carmel.

Duckworth's gamble did not pay off, as the railroad line extension plans were abandoned. Nevertheless, Santiago Duckworth began advertising "Carmel City" in 1889. Several houses and a small hotel were built. Despite Duckworth's efforts, sales were slow.

Duckworth was joined by new sales agent partner, Abbie J. Hunter, marketing parcels along this dry barren stretch of coast. After near bankruptcy, Duckworth decided to sell out. His partner Hunter survived financially because of her bathhouse on the beach at the end of what became Ocean Avenue.

It was in 1889 that the name, *Carmel-by-the-Sea* was first written on a postcard flyer issued by bathhouse owner Abbie J. Hunter.

In 1902, not the least bit aware of any preeminent vision, Duckworth walked into the office of the visionary who in years earlier had been enamored with Carmel: Frank Devendorf. His office in San Jose held rights to similar development parcels in the prosperous river landing commercial community of Stockton which interested Duckworth.

They made the trade and Frank Powers, a prominent San Francisco attorney, joined Devendorf upon recommendations by mutual friends. Together the two Franks went on to form the Carmel Development Company.

While Duckworth was confounded by the railroad's failure to extend its line to his beach-side community, Devendorf would revel in the lack of a carnival-like atmosphere. Carmel-by-the-Sea would evoke privacy. This particular virtue sustains its village character to this day.

Frank Devendorf's picnic view of Carmel.

Color, texture and the use of wood and stone contribute to Carmel's` charm and sense of permanence.

Carmel's summer fog hangs over the downtown district —which has the feel of a northern European village.

*Stone, clay, wood and tile—a marriage of
natural materials.*

Hand-crafted construction blends well with the natural environment.

23

Color, light and other visual delights are to be found around every corner throughout the downtown.

ARTS AND CRAFTS MOVEMENT

During the early days of development in Carmel, a group of architects and designers focused their attentions on the problems of industrial mass production. The proponents of this cause developed a mentality more like artists than their architect predecessors. They called for a return to honest and superior design and craftmanship.

The whole world was undergoing a cultural change. Industrial life promoted by big business was confronted by rustic artists. The building industry was offering prefabricated houses which were produced in factories with poor working conditions.

The opposition Arts and Crafts movement was spearheaded by craftsman and editor Gustav Stickly who promoted the philosophy of hand-crafted construction. All the nature-nurture architects, such as Bernard Maybeck, brothers Greene and Greene and a young Frank Lloyd Wright were in protest against the industrial life. They were all advocates of building with natural materials to enhance nature with the presence of mankind.

There was a belief in a link between declining social morals and the plush luxuries of the Victorian life-style. As Stickly wrote in 1909, "*When luxury enters in, and a thousand artificial requirements come to be regarded as real needs, the nation is on the brink of degeneration.*" Industrial structures of disposable products brought about planned obsolescence and some also thought disposable relationships.

The *Craftsman* and other similar magazines that promoted the naturalist life-style railed against the prefabricated and mass-produced materials of interstate commerce. These publications showed uses for natural materials usually found on site. Unpretentious cottage plans were published and became available to the general populace for the price of a single magazine. These new ideas caught the imagination of individuals desiring a more simple life. The opinions in these magazines blended perfectly with the vision of Carmel's founding fathers.

Woodworking craftsmen, masons, and other hand-craft builders saw hope for economic recovery in growing demands for their skills again. These contestants of industry would herald the skilled arts and crafts of building: stone masonry, fine woodwork and ironwork in their designs. Those who were encouraged to take up hand-craft professions brought to life the Carmel community arts and crafts industry. The movement's link between *building* and *family values* prompted visionaries like Frank Devendorf to create simple communities based on traditional values.

In Carmel it was the promise of a newly designed community that fostered the likes of Francis Whittaker who engaged in foundry art work. Architects like Julia Morgan and Charles Greene and eccentrics like Hugh Comstock added to the architectural metamorphosis. Builders such as M.J. Murphy, Gottfried, Bowen and Hale made use of the natural materials to incorporate patterned utilitarian designs.

These builders and architects used wood from coastal forests, stone from nearby quarries and constructed buildings that incorporated furniture into the walls and closets. Many of these homes became historically designated structures and are still evident in today's Carmel.

The Arts and Crafts phenomenon coincided with early building in Carmel and launched a development philosophy in Carmel that still remains to this day.

World War I monument designed by Carmel architect Charles Sumner Greene.

The artistic use of stone is common in both residential and commercial construction.

29

Born of fire and earth, tile provides a visual accent blending well with Carmel's architectural style.

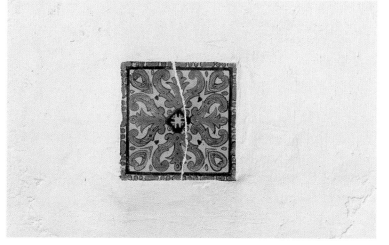

Works by Carmel artists and artisans are showcased throughout the village.

The allure of the ocean is always strong in this coastal village.

33

This manicured home was designed by architect Julia Morgan in 1940 for a married couple she knew as an undergraduate student. Redwood was used liberally throughout the interior and exterior of the house which included built-in furniture.

The Harrison Memorial Library, built in 1927-1928, was a joint effort of architect Bernard Maybeck as interpreted by local builder M.J. Murphy.

Carmel's master builder M.J. Murphy built his first home in 1902 at the age of seventeen. In the 1990's, the house was saved by Carmel Heritage and was actually raised by a crane and moved to a new spot close to the library. It now serves as a town community center.

The temperate climate of Carmel allows colorful gardens to flourish year round.

CARMEL — TOWN GROWTH

Frank Devendorf's plan for Carmel included attracting people to the community who shared his vision. With his partner, Frank Powers, they set about to create a town that reflected the Arts and Crafts movement philosophy—of people living in harmony with nature.

Devendorf came from a family of visionaries. One of his relatives was a developer who had founded Saratoga Springs, the New York spa community. Frank possessed a competitive drive coupled with profound sense of honor and an obsession for nature and health.

Frank Powers was very much a Teddy Roosevelt-like outdoors man with a sentimental side. He was a hard-working, health conscious and wealthy city dweller. His wife was an artist who revelled in the beauty of the natural landscape. The Powers brought optimism to the project.

The two Franks would ponder their situation. Devendorf came up with an expression for those whom they wanted to settle and develop their community—brain workers. In his first sales brochure, Devendorf appealed directly to California school teachers. He offered inexpensive accommodations at the refurbished Pine Inn, bargain land prices and generous payment terms. Deals were consummated to attract people, who readily came.

While Frank Powers died in 1920, never getting to fully enjoy his colony, Devendorf lived to the ripe old age of 78 and was the primary force in Carmel's early development.

Under Devendorf's direction, Carmel began to take form. Duckworth's original street grid plan was quickly modified to conform to the natural terrain. Roads were realigned and curved to harmonize better with trees, slopes and to improve drainage. Devendorf's Carmel may have been the first community in the West to give nature such respect.

Devendorf realized the need for trees for aesthetics and to curb erosion. He eventually planted hundreds of trees particularly along Ocean Avenue. Most of the land of the original Carmel Development Company was barren and dry. All the trees, with the exception of some pines, redwood trees (now mostly felled for building) and some oak trees, were planted by residents and benefactors. Local residents became the keepers of the trees, the cultivators of local flora. The community attitude in Carmel seemed to foster an appreciation of natural landscape and a continuing community conscience to care for and maintain the local vegetation.

Devendorf originally paid Japanese workers to lead his horse down Ocean Avenue with barrels of water to keep all the trees alive. It gave the impression that in Carmel there was abundant water. In fact, Carmel's water supply pipeline from nearby Pebble Beach was rather unreliable in the early years. It later relied upon a horse-drawn supply system.

Despite attractive prices, buyers were slow to respond to Carmel's natural beauty. Frank Devendorf's finances were severely strained as he persevered in promoting his community vision. His idea of attracting "brain workers" gained ground when U.S. surveyor David Starr Jordan bought property in Carmel. His relationships with professors at the University of California and Stanford University served to popularize Carmel with the academic staff. An area of homes near the beach even became known as "Faculty Row."

Life in Carmel remained fairly primitive. Wind would blow sand inside houses and the sounds of nature were loud. Drownings off Carmel Beach were not uncommon. Common fears generated by the closeness of nature kept Carmel from growing at a quicker pace.

* * *

Cheap land, attractive financing, the natural life-style and scenic beauty had great appeal to Bohemians from San Francisco—to artists, writers, poets, musicians and painters. Frank Powers used his position in the San Francisco community to promote his seaside development. At Coppa's Restaurant, a popular Bohemian gathering place, poet George Sterling heard the call. Sterling, known as the "King of Bohemia," would later describe Carmel as, *"a true bohemian grove filled with light and the sound of waves, the scent of the ocean in every breeze."*

In 1905, George Sterling left San Francisco for a simpler life in the woods of Carmel. His bungalow amidst the groves of Carmel began to replace the usual Bohemian gathering places. The Coppa's crowd began migrating south. Arriving were writers, playwrights and poets, many from San Francisco and others from the east coast. Individuals such as photographer Arnold Genthe came and stayed, while others like writer Jack London visited briefly. Those who stayed invited others. Visitors such as London wrote about the gathering of talent and the naturalist life-style. Word spread and soon Carmel had earned the reputation as an artist colony. Many others moved to Carmel including James Hopper, Lincoln Steffans, Upton Sinclair and later poet Robinson Jeffers and his wife Una.

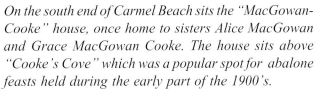

On the south end of Carmel Beach sits the "MacGowan-Cooke" house, once home to sisters Alice MacGowan and Grace MacGowan Cooke. The house sits above "Cooke's Cove" which was a popular spot for abalone feasts held during the early part of the 1900's.

Mary Austin Park was dedicated in memory of writer and Carmel resident Mary Austin.

Author Mary Austin bought a plot and built a tree house in Carmel (she called it a wick-i-up.) She wrote at a table located on the tree house deck. From her publishing profits, Austin was successful enough to purchase several lots that are now known and preserved as Mary Austin Park. Her lovely cottage that replaced the tree house remains in this grove as an edifice to the successful art and writings that originated in Carmel.

Writers and sisters Alice MacGowan and Grace MacGowan Cooke followed Upton Sinclair from New Jersey and purchased a lofty white Cape Cod style home on Carmel beach at the end of 13th Avenue. Local residents popularized this stretch of beach with their abalone picnics. Partly because of the conspicuousness of the house, this section of Carmel Beach became known as Cooke's Cove.

Other luminaries added to Carmel lore. Sinclair Lewis worked in Carmel as a secretary copying manuscripts. Lewis' own writings sold well when he was in London and the published novelist returned to live on 7th Avenue in downtown Carmel.

The carefree life-style for Sterling and his followers included seafood picnics on the beach with songs about abalone. A carefree club of creative people gathered here—their only ticket for admission being the creation of a verse about abalone. Over 90 different abalone song verses were created over the years.

* * *

In 1910 the local newspaper, the *Carmel Pine Cone*, reported Berkeley editor and University Professor Perry Newberry's visit with a glowing biography. Devendorf, eager to entice him into his community personally ushered Newberry around to view all the choicest lots.

Leading Newberry in front of a lot with two trees, Devendorf, made an unprecedented offer of $5.00 down and $5.00 a month with no payments or interest for one year. When Newberry humbly nodded his agreement, Devendorf put up the sold sign near the property line of the second lot and pronounced that the sale was to include an option on the second lot for no extra cost. That meant Newberry had both lots.

Perry Newberry went on to become a devoted Carmel resident, who promoted the festive life-style of the area. Running on the anti-commercial motto "*If you truly want Carmel to become a boosting, hustling, wide-awake lively metropolis, DON'T VOTE FOR PERRY NEWBERRY*," he became one of Carmel's more notable politicians. He also served as editor of the very *Pine Cone* newspaper that raved about him when he first came to visit.

Unlike many other communities, there was a focus to all the creative energies flowing through Carmel. A community spirit was brought to life centering around theater and music. Herbert "Bert" Heron founded the outdoor Forest Theater in 1910. Thus began the tradition of amateur community productions of original plays. Most of the well known residents of early Carmel performed or assisted at the Theater at one time or another. The theater became a creative link bringing all segments of the community together.

In 1924, Edward Kuster built the Golden Bough Theater complex for more professional dramatic productions. Although the theater burned down in 1935 after a performance of the play *By Candlelight*, the other adjacent buildings live on as the Court of the Golden Bough. Coincidently, Kuster's Studio Theatre of the Golden Bough burned down in 1949 after a performance of *By Candlelight*.

Musician Dene Denny and artist Hazel Watrous moved to Carmel in the 1920's and began

building houses in Carmel Woods. In 1935, the two women organized a concert series including a three day Bach Festival. So popular was the Bach portion of the series, that in future years it was expanded. The annual Bach Festival is now an international music event.

With inexpensive living costs and a prospering community spirit, Carmel began to grow. Carmel was incorporated as a township in 1916. Numerous laws were adopted to preserve the residential and rustic character of the town. One such law was the absolute prohibition against the cutting of trees without city permission. Since it is estimated there are currently more than 35,000 trees in Carmel, this law would have to be judged a great success. Many other laws followed aimed at preserving the unique character of this coastal community.

In 1929, more than twenty years after the Development Company partnership was born, City Attorney Argyll Campbell drafted the community Magna Charta, as he boldly called it. "*The City of Carmel-by-the-Sea,*" his ordinance declared, "*is hereby determined to be...predominantly a residential city wherein business and commerce...are...subordinated to its residential character.*" Community protectiveness became an ongoing theme. Over the course of Carmel's history, many legal battles have been fought about the town's character.

In Frank Devendorf's later years, he was asked what he thought about Carmel's offbeat nature. He responded that he was glad that he sold land cheap to poets and painters who were happy to plant his trees...he was glad Carmel turned out the way it did...he was rooting for the poets against the businessmen to keep it that way.

Two trees fronting the original home of Perry Newberry.

The Seven Arts Building created by Herbert (Bert) Heron in 1925 has housed many popular businesses and art-related establishments.

The historic Pine Inn shown from the beach side: Santiago Duckworth's original Hotel Carmelo was put on rollers and moved down Ocean Avenue to the corner of Lincoln Street. Frank Devendorf expanded it with the help of M.J. Murphy and renamed it the Pine Inn. The original hotel forms part of the Pine Inn as it stands today.

Artistic adornment in commercial and residential structures demonstrates the great importance of the arts for this community.

49

Carmel Plaza during the Bach Festival. The town approval of Carmel Plaza took over 10 years. The Plaza development became an issue which pitted Carmel's commercial and residential interests against each other determining the direction of the town's future character.

The ancient craft of stone masonry has been practiced in Carmel since its earliest days.

Merchants take pride in their establishments through the use of simple ornament.

Carmel is well known for its fine dining and cuisine.

Trees have first priority in Carmel. Businesses and pedestrian traffic must adjust to the existing natural environment.

Evening at the Cypress Inn.

A rainy day at the historic Pine Inn which has an interesting history dating back to Carmel's earliest days in the 1800's.

REGULATIONS

Without residential mail delivery in Carmel, homes developed names—not numbers.

From the beginning, laws were meant to retain Carmel's integrity. Some laws enacted included the prohibition against: tall buildings, sidewalks in residential areas, electric signs, residential street lights, the selling of muffins in a cookie shop, the wearing of high heels and the selling of ice cream. The high heel ban resulted after Carmel was sued by a woman in high heels who had fallen.

In 1985 Council action prohibiting the relocation of water use permits resulted in a de facto "ice cream ban" in Carmel. As a result, the town was called "Scrooge City." Many felt that those in power had gone too far with their antibusiness agendas.

From the earliest days of plantings by Devendorf, trees have held a special place for Carmel's residents. All trees have been inventoried and no tree on public or private property may be removed without permission of the City. Individuals damaging trees can be severely fined.

As a result of the residential sidewalk ban (because it would mean cutting trees for sidewalks), the United States Postal Service refused rural mail delivery. With no other use for house numbers besides mail delivery, privacy and intimacy flourished in the village. Most houses have names but no numbers for identification.

POST OFFICE

In this artists' town without rural postal delivery, the Post Office centered as a gathering point for artists and writers. According to long time resident, Jehan Salenger-Carlson a San Francisco newspaper art critic, a special slang developed among writers regarding their manuscripts' return or acceptance. If material submitted was returned it was "a thick," and nobody would say anything. If it was "a thin," the expression meant a check came, or a contract or letter, usually some communication of acceptance. The whole village population would generally know about this artistic success. Carmel remains a community that revolves around the Post Office.

MAYORS AND LEADERS OF CARMEL

Carmel has attracted numerous personalities over the years beginning with its earliest days as an artist colony. With so many strong-willed individuals living in close proximity to each other, it was inevitable that these people would be attracted to politics as a means to promote their particular vision for Carmel.

No more heartfelt persons have ever claimed the title of mayor anywhere in the world than Carmel mayors. From actor and Forest Theater founder came mayor Herbert (Bert) Heron. Heron's Forest Theater lays claim to being the state's first outdoor theater. Visitors arrived from all parts of California to view original performances outdoors surrounded by Carmel's trees.

In the 1950's, 1960's and again in the 1970's there was Gunnar Norberg, whose passionate anti-growth style earned him many supporters and detractors. During his term of office, the Carmel Sunset School (home to the Carmel Bach Festival) was saved. That action gave us the refitted fine art center dedicated to art workshops and gallery exhibitions. Today it retains the name of the Sunset Center. Norberg's 1970's campaign centered around saving the Forest Theater.

That campaign also started the political career of photographer Ed Weston's young son Cole, a trained actor and theater director. Cole became Carmel's first congressional candidate and later became the Executive Director of the Sunset Cultural Center. Cole Weston ran the workshop facility and opened the door for the foundation of the globally known "Friends of Photography" whose membership included photographers Brett Weston, Ansel Adams and Wynn Bullock.

The town changed with Norberg's attempted reelection in 1968. Barney Laiolo successfully contested Norberg and became the mayor of Carmel. Laiolo had a more balanced approach to development than his predecessor. He was also dedicated to eliminating much of Carmel's bureaucracy. He might have succeeded had it not been for the cultural revolution that invaded Carmel in the 1960's and the anti-drug programs that were necessary.

The Mayor devoted much of his own precious time, seated undercover on park benches trying to curb drug sales. There were few police in the village. A town that emphasized art and fine craftsmanship left crime fighting low on the budgetary ladder. Norberg and Laiolo remained adversaries in Carmel politics throughout the 1970's and into the 1980's.

In the 1980's, forbidden from building a commercial structure, Carmel's famous resident Clint Eastwood became incensed. He spoke with quiet articulation on his own behalf at a town business association meeting one day. From that calm display of diplomatic and political know-how, his neighbors drafted him for election in 1986, and he became known as Carmel's great negotiator mayor.

Eastwood calmly took over where his ex-mayor neighbor Laiolo had left off. One of Eastwood's first acts as mayor, causing a great deal of consternation, was to dismiss six planning commissioners. During his time as mayor, the city had a more permissive attitude towards commercial projects than previous administrations. Under Mayor Eastwood, a long overdue public restroom was added to the park and the Carmel Youth Center was rejuvenated. From a vacating bank, Eastwood negotiated for a children's library and vaulted local history depository which contains photos, posters, books and manuscripts going back to Carmel's early days. The "ice cream ban" was also subsequently dropped.

Carmel-by-the-Sea City Hall.

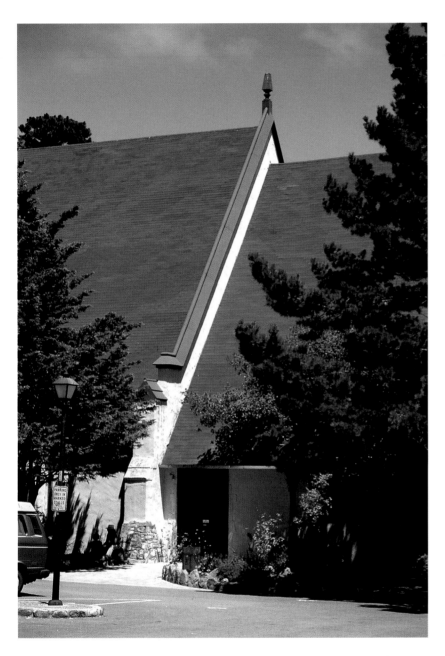

The Sunset Center was originally the site of Carmel's Sunset School started in1903. The auditorium, designed by architect C.J. Ryland, served the school's and community's needs until the 1960's when the school needed more room. As a result of a 1964 City bond issue, the school was saved and became the site of the Sunset Cultural Center, housing workshops for the arts and gallery exhibitions. The Center continues to be used for symphony performances and the Carmel Bach Festival.

The famous Hog's Breath Inn Restaurant is popular with tourists and locals alike.

The Carmel Dairy building, now home to the Mediterranean Market was built in the 1930's. The interior walls were originally painted with murals by local artist Jo Mora.

65

Interesting architecture and inviting sitting areas may be discovered around every bend.

The creative use of lines and texture distinguish this coastal town.

67

Care is given to every detail of this tiled stairway and passageway.

Even a public water fountain is not left unadorned.

69

Village Corner

the
IMPULSE
SHOPPES

miniatures
original art
imported giftware

DOLL HOUSES

SUMMER SALE

SUMMER SALE

Walkways and sidewalks go around precious trees.

Narrow alleys attract the curious visitor and inspire a sense of wonder and discovery.

A hidden courtyard and secret garden awaits exploration.

The romantic La Playa Hotel was originally designed by Christian Jorgensen in 1902 as a mansion. It was the first home in Carmel to have a swimming pool. The building was later expanded and converted into a hotel. Some of the original stonework of the mansion is still visible.

CARMEL'S ARCHITECTURE

Carmel's design and building philosophy grew out of the Arts and Crafts movement. As architectural trends changed over time, all forms of building designs found their way to Carmel. The old fashioned millionaire's playhouse bungalow gave way to the mini-mansion.

Carmel became built up with every sort of design imaginable. Architects often had unlimited resources, as did some who were asked to experiment with no budget at all. Architectural styles varied from Box Modern in the 1950's, Haciendito style out of the Mission architecture, Mediterranean styles and Arab stucco designs. There were ranch, mixed with Cape Cod barn homes and southern mansion miniatures. Also built were driftwood homes and stone castles, a Vermont ski lodge and A-frames. Japanese Country Cottage style and Chinese Toy houses nestle well in the trees near English Tudor, Summerset, Western Ranch and French Chateau Gate houses.

Endless styles appeared in Carmel, most adhering to the ideas of the town's earliest builders: to blend in with and respect the natural environment.

* * *

Conjuring, criticizing, arguing and praising an openhearted human ethic in the 1920's through our second World War years, was self-made mason architect—poet Robinson Jeffers. With the construction of Tor House by M.J. Murphy, Jeffers learned "the art of making stone love stone." As an act of love and passion for his wife Una, Jeffers later built Hawk Tower from stones he collected. The unique tower provides views of nearby Carmel Bay and contains a secret passageway. In 1978, the Tor House Foundation purchased the property to preserve the buildings and collections. It is open to the public on a limited basis.

A most unique builder and designer was non-architect Hugh Comstock. He built his fantasy designs in Carmel starting in 1924 that have become synonymous for Carmel charm. Comstock's wife made rag dolls. Her dolls were in such numbers, strewn around their Carmel house, that Hugh decided to build a small cottage from a child's book drawing in order to house these dolls.

Working from "the hip" with no drawn plans, Comstock first built Hansel House. Soon, visiting family members and friends forced him to build again. He built another doll house next door as a second guest house. It was named the Gretel house. Comstock then built a home for himself on Torres. When it sold quickly, he built what became his own residence

Robinson Jeffers' Hawk Tower and Tor House:
Many of the stones used were gathered from
various locations as far away as Europe. From the
lookout turret of Hawk Tower, there were views
of Carmel Bay, Point Lobos to the south and the
Del Monte Forest to the north.

around the corner. Still without written plans, Comstock built his daughter's home across the street from his own; it was the fourth of seventeen original Comstock houses to be constructed in Carmel. Later, as a commercial builder, Comstock built the Tuck Box, designed after an old English tea house.

Edward Kuster is sometimes credited with building Carmel's first fairy tale style building with his Court of the Golden Bough Theater complex which opened in 1924.

Among young masons were Italians like DeAngelo who worked first for master builder M.J. Murphy. Murphy was well known for his fine workmanship and contributed numerous buildings to Carmel's heritage including the Harrison Memorial Library (designed by Bernard Maybeck) and portions of Frank Devendorf's Pine Inn. Local builder L.E. Gottfried also contributed to Carmel's development. He was followed by a number of idealistic developers.

Architect Charles Sumner Greene, who with his brother Henry (Greene and Greene) are well known for their "bungalow" architectural style during the early part of the century, actually moved to Carmel in 1915. A number of homes in the region were designed by Charles Greene including his own studio located a short distance from downtown Carmel.

In his later years, Frank Lloyd Wright designed a residence at the southern end of Carmel Beach built upon basaltic lava rocks. The home, built in 1954, is said to look like the upside-down hull of a ship.

In 1940, architect Julia Morgan added to the mix by designing a retirement cottage in Carmel for a couple she knew. During construction, she was known to walk to Carmel from her own cottage located in Monterey.

One home was started by a man from Chicago named Ralph Seymor. His expectations for living in the California sunshine were dashed when, over the course of several summers, the fog rarely lifted. He sold his house incompletely built. It was later completed by others.

* * *

Only one vacant lot remains within the one square mile of the original Carmel-by-the-Sea development parcels. It is still owned by the family who purchased it from Devendorf's Carmel Development Company many years ago. Incidentally, there is a bird house in a tree on that lot.

Hugh Comstock's Tuck Box Tea Room (now a restaurant) built in 1926 showcases his unique architectural style which has become synonymous with Carmel.

79

Homes by Hugh Comstock

One of Hugh Comstock's "fairy tale" adobe homes.

The historic Mission Ranch, established in 1850 near Carmel Mission, was saved from possible demolition and restored by actor Clint Eastwood in 1986. The Mission Ranch now serves as an inn and restaurant (below).

Stone house built by Carmel builder M.J. Murphy (above).

The Soto House, the only remaining home from the "Tortilla Flats" area of Carmel, was built in 1907. The house, owned by Maria Soto (Mamacita) was home to as many as twenty wayward children. At least one murder occurred at the residence (right).

This Frank Lloyd Wright-designed house was modeled after an upside-down ship hull. The home was built in 1954 on the southern side of Carmel Beach. The durable copper roof blends well with the seaside surroundings.

Residents of Carmel place a high value on privacy. Homes are designed and landscaped with privacy in mind.

Bus stop in a residential neighborhood.

Many different styles have made their way into Carmel's rich architectural metamorphosis.

Carmel cottage interior. Note the liberal use of redwood throughout (left).

Old shutters—rustic hand-crafted simplicity.

90

Creative landscaping provides natural privacy.

93

94

Laws aimed at protecting the residential character of the town have encouraged growth in a slow timeless manner.

Good materials create lasting places.

Meandering pathways weave through residential districts. Plants and trees thrive under the watchful eye of local residents.

A symbiotic relationship between man and nature.

Carmel's residents have traditionally taken on the role of "keepers of the trees," the protectors of local flora and fauna.

103

Homes have been built with respect for these
ancient sentinels of time—trees.

The line between public and private is usually quite clear.

Private entries.

Cottage of light (left).

Cottage of shadow (left).

109

Trees and homes intermingled—a natural place...a timeless place.

Street windows serve as a visual portal connecting life inside with the outside.

Small details are reflective of a community pride in their heritage.

A cypress tree embraces a Carmel home (left).

Numerous architectural styles abound in Carmel.

Mary Austin built her tree platform in 1906 and then others followed suit.

With his goal of developing a family oriented community, Frank Devendorf donated two lots in 1905 on Lincoln Avenue near Ocean Avenue for the First Methodist Episcopal Church of Carmel. The building is now known as the Church of the Wayfarer.

Hansel House

Gretel House

***

Carmel—a timeless place
in a tumultuous world